MAKING TIME

THE I LIKE TO MAKE STUFF STORY

BOB CLAGETT

CONTENTS

INTRODUCTION

Who is this book for?

I get questions on almost a daily basis about how I got started making videos on the internet and when I started making things. I hear from lots of people who would like to do those things too, but they don't know where to start. Some of them have started but don't fully understand what it's like to create content full time, or what steps are necessary to turn their hobby into a career.

I can't claim to answer all of those questions, because I think the path is different for everyone. However, this book is my attempt to share my path and experience with others so that they can be informed and encouraged as they strike out on a new adventure.

This book was written almost exclusively on airplanes and in airports over the course of two years. I wrote for a couple of hours every few months while I travelled to and from work events. If it seems to evolve as you read it, that's because it did, and I did as well. A lot changed in those two years, and I hope it shows in the writing.

I hope this book can give you some perspective on what it took for me to become a full time content creator, and I sincerely hope you enjoy it!
    -Bob

PART 1

Hi, I'm Bob and I like to make stuff. I always have. As a kid, I made castles and forts from cardboard boxes. I made everything I could think of with Lego, Construx, Lincoln Logs and Tinker Toys. My first snowboard was a piece of 3/4″ plywood with the corners cut at 45° angles and velcro straps (stolen from my Mom's sewing materials) running through the board. I made a bow and arrow from a piece of oak tongue and groove flooring, using weed whacker line as the string. The arrow was a wooden dowel with a repurposed dart tip on the end.

One of my favorite things was to use toys to make other toys that I didn't have. For example, I LOVED Star Wars growing up (I still do) but didn't have all of the ships for my action figures. As a way around that, I used Lego bricks to temporarily make the vehicles that I wanted to play with. Stacked up cardboard boxes, connected by cutout trap doors gave me bigger castles and bases than were even available in the stores, all for free, from the back of a grocery store. It was a way to create what I needed in the moment, without a permanent investment on the part of my parents every time a new toy came out. I didn't realize it at the time, but that was forcing me to problem solve and create with what was at hand.

I didn't even think of it as a "thing" to make stuff, it was just what I did. That was mostly due to the fact that I was surrounded by people who weren't afraid to construct and to fix things. My "Pa" was a contractor, who built a lot of McDonald's restaurants, smoked a pipe, drove a pickup truck and had a shop full of tools. My "Grandad" was a jack of all trades. He was a dentist, a painter, wood carver, RC plane builder and all around incredible person. My dad inherited the "jack of all trades" gene (and passed it to me, I guess) from Grandad and has always built, fixed or created the things we needed. He let me hang in his shop and watch him build things at a young age, and most importantly of all, he gave me the opportunity to try things. I had access to space, some materials and limited tools to create.

Let me explain to you the kind of parents I was blessed enough to grow up with, as the youngest of three children. When I was around 12 or 13, my parents asked my older siblings what they should do differently in my teenage years. My brother and sister responded (something to the effect of) "back off. Give him freedom to make mistakes." They did.

Granted, I was a pretty good kid and didn't cause much trouble, but they took a chance and gave me the freedom to build things IN our house and use the space in a way that most of my friends couldn't fathom. As an example, some friends and I scavenged a bunch of plywood scraps from construction sites around town (stuff from the burn pile) and built a quarter pipe skateboard ramp... IN my basement. As it turned out, it was bigger than the door, so we had to cut it in half to get it outside. My parents didn't say a negative word to me about it. After that, I built a set of 8 ft. climbing wall panels and wrapped three walls with them. Again, not a hint of negative response.

The climbing wall panels ended up becoming a stage when my high school rock band played our first show, in my basement, to 80-90 kids. To my complete surprise, my parents helped me take the $1 admission at our front door. They didn't complain about the noise, mess and smell that came with that many teenagers, most of whom they didn't know.

This is where I came from, and as a parent myself.. it's what I want to create for my kids. I want to provide them the skills and freedom to explore, make, fail and explore again.

Side note: It's very easy to fall into the trap of trying to pacify our kids by giving them what they want most of the time, but giving them raw materials and the freedom to create is probably the better gift in the long term. In our house, we separate out unsafe recyclables (glass, sharp cans, etc) and everything else goes in a bin that my kids have full access to. They also have an infinite supply of tape (and boy, do they go through it). Great things are made when creative kids have the materials to exercise their imagination.

WHEN I WAS FINISHING high school, I was planning on going to University of Kentucky for graphic design, which was not a particularly strong program. At the last minute, I came up with a presentation to give to my parents. The idea was that I would get an art scholarship and attend the Savannah College of Art and Design, in Savannah, GA.

They went for it. All I had to do was get a portfolio scholarship.

The only issue was that I was in my senior year of high school and had very little material for a portfolio to show off.

My art teacher, Mrs. Shipp, had a huge impact on me during my final two years of high school. She encouraged me to pursue art and since I didn't have a portfolio, she let me modify my assignments as a way to build a "fake" portfolio. By that I mean that she allowed me to change assignments so that each project was intentionally unique. This gave me a very broad scope of work, both in materials and techniques, which made for a robust portfolio. She taught me to create work outside of my natural skillset simply to build a wide collection to show off.

I got a scholarship, and off I went.

My plan, at the beginning of college, was to get a degree in graphic design, specifically because I was assuming that it was computer aided design. When I took my first GD class, the professor said "this is an intro class. No computers.. only paper, pencils and rulers." It was a fundamental class, to teach the roots of the art before we could use the newer tools on the computers. Of course, now, I understand it's value, but as an 18 year old who was distracted by everything, it was enough reason for me to switch majors, to Computer Art.

IN THOSE DAYS, Computer Art was really a survey of how computers were used in lots of different fields. We got trained in some 3d modeling and animation, basic motion graphics, sound design and video production, as well as general design and layout software (mostly Photoshop and Illustrator). It was too early (late 1990's) to be taught any web programming in college. What wasn't available to me in class, I found on the, relatively young, internet. When I did take an html class near the end of school, the professor wouldn't let me write the code manually. I had to use Dreamweaver for a drag and drop experience.

Around this time, I had begun to work with friend of mine building websites for local businesses. We started a small company and worked at it to try to generate some money. This all happened from midnight to 3AM for months while trying to finish school.

IN MY LAST two quarters of college, the school introduced Interactive Design and Gaming Design classes, so I jumped right on those opportunities. In my final quarter of school, I took an Interactive Design class from one of the best professors I'd had all throughout school. On the last day of class, she pulled me aside and took me to the dean.

He told me how she was leaving the school, and suggested that I take over her position and teach the class (starting in one week, right after spring break). I took the job, and was able to teach for two quarters, while our young company grew enough to be able to pay our rent. At the time, although I really enjoyed the teaching, I mostly saw it as a steady income while I grew a business. Looking back, I see that it was my first introduction to teaching people things that I had only just learned myself. Something I do to this day.

ANOTHER INTERESTING THING about last part of my college experience was again, faking a portfolio. In the last quarter (or semester) of senior year at an art school, everyone has to take a portfolio class. It's a class simply focused on creating a good presentation of your best work from years of school.

For most of us computer art majors, that meant creating a demo reel full of animation, motion graphics as well as mixed in images of print work. I'd been focusing so heavily on the available interactive design classes that I had very little of those types of work to show. My interactive pieces (mostly done in Director) were already packaged and easy to show off. To pass the class, I needed a "reel" so that my professor had something to grade. He tasked me with faking it. He told me to use the class as a chance to learn enough of the tools to fake a demo reel by creating tiny examples of work. Usually, students had to grab the most compelling parts of their work to put into a reel, but I got to create 2-3 seconds of compelling stuff over and over until I had a full reel worth. This was hugely important to me long term and yet another example of being able to create on the fly. During this quarter of school, I learned how to use After Effects to create motion graphics. I learned video editing well enough to collate the pieces. It gave me a foundation for creating videos from nothing.

AFTER I'D FINISHED my short teaching career, our company continued to grow for several years. We built a team of really amazing, talented friends and did work for other agencies and brands.

DURING THESE YEARS, I'd been in a dating relationship that was, well, safe. I settled into an imagined future that seemed like it was smart and stable. Over the years of that relationship, I set aside a lot of my creative pursuits to focus on creating a stable life that my girlfriend's parents would approve of.

That relationship ended abruptly and all of the plans I'd been making around it were up in the air.

HERE'S A PERSONAL STORY, unrelated to the purpose of this book.

My girlfriend and I broke up on a Thursday morning, after 3 years. I was confused and upset but not really sad, just shellshocked. I talked to a good friend the next day about going somewhere for the weekend, just to get away and clear my head. He was chaperoning a college ski trip for our church and invited me to come along.

On Friday morning, I pulled up to the parking lot with a bag full of snow gear. The first person I saw in the parking lot was my wife.

We met that weekend and immediately connected in a way that I hadn't thought possible. She wasn't caught up in appearances and didn't care about things being safe and stable. She was fun, crazy and something I'd never experienced. We started hanging out the next week, got engaged 6 months later, then married 8 months after that. 15 years later, she's still fun, confident and a perfect counter to the parts of me that need to play it safe. She's a roller derby playing, mother of four who serves others and cares for everyone she meets. She's awesome.

TWO YEARS after we got married, we bought our first home, which came with a pretty large detached garage. I had the time, freedom and space to build out a fantastic workshop. I rebuilt a couple of vintage Vespa scooters and built several pieces of furniture. The house was old and came with lots of projects as well. I learned a lot from owning our first house, including how to build a 400 sq ft deck with wrap around steps. I learned to replace windows and re tile floors there. I also learned that paint colors are not worth arguing about. My wife picks the paint now.

AFTER 5 OR 6 years running our company, one of the agencies that we worked with offered to buy us out, which came as a relief. The stress of responsibility for the paychecks of good friends can get exhausting. We came in under the agency, as their "interactive" department and did several years of really good work.

ABOUT A YEAR after selling our company to the agency, my wife and I had our first child, and moved into a larger house about nine months later. Unfortunately, the new house didn't have a dedicated workshop. At the time, it was a reasonable thing to let go of. Kids need bedrooms, not garages. I moved all of my tools into my rather large office room and put them in containers. If I needed to use them, I just took them outside. With a young child, we intentionally bought a house that didn't need any real work. In those first few years, there weren't many reasons to pull my tools out of the containers.

IT WAS during my time at the ad agency that I decided to move my old website (with a horrible name) to a new domain. One random afternoon I sat down to search for a new domain and one of my first thoughts was, "well, I like to make stuff... but surely that's not available." Oddly, *iliketomakestuff.com* was. I immediately bought it with no real intention of using it for anything specific. I moved my site there and moved on with life.

After almost four years, our new bosses wanted to consolidate office locations and informed us that we would all start commuting an hour each way to the company headquarters. That was the same day I started looking for a new job. With a young son at home, I had zero interest in losing that much of my life to a commute.

I was blessed to quickly find a new job, building new software products for Dell, working from home. I went from producing marketing media for products (that I wouldn't recommend to a friend) to building applications that made it easier for people to do their jobs. This was a significant change in how I valued my work. It wasn't making a global difference, or affecting things on a huge scale, but it was helpful to a very specific group of people. One of the biggest things about it that I realize now, was that I was making a new thing from scratch. It was a product that didn't exist before I took the job.

MY WIFE and I had 3 more children in the course of 5 years. Our family grew considerably in a relatively short period of time. The responsibility at home grew larger and my free time grew smaller. During that time, I got antsy and generally overwhelmed.

I found myself, working from home, a hollow core door

away from young kids. I enjoyed my work, completely adored my kids, but had no buffer between the two. I had no commute, or separation, for my mind to clear of one thing before being filled up with another. I needed a hobby and the most natural thing at the time was music.

I hadn't played any music in several years, since right before my oldest son was born when my band of several years dissolved. Unfortunately, part of having several young kids is that being in a band, practicing, and playing shows wasn't very realistic anymore. YouTube gave me a way to play music, without ever having to leave my house.

MUSIC

Around 2007/2008 Jack Conte (of Pomplamoose and now, Patreon) started a YouTube video trend called the "Video-Song." He explained the idea like this:

VIDEOSONG, a new medium with two rules:

    1. What you see is what you hear (no lip-syncing for instruments or voice).

    2. If you hear it, at some point you see it (no hidden sounds).

I LOVED THE IDEA, and watching Jack's music was more than enough inspiration for me to give it a try. I still had all of my old equipment from my band days. I spent some time (and cash from freelance work) gathering up a few more things until I had everything I needed to write, perform, record and publish my own music to YouTube in this new VideoSong format.

    In the end, I only recorded two of these full songs

myself, but the more important part for me, was realizing what YouTube actually was. In my mind, I had previously thought of YouTube as a place to look up old tv commercials, watch people complain about things or watch cat videos. Instead, I found that it was actually a community of communities. It was a place filled with groups of people who shared common interests and ideas, but rather than being spun out into their own websites, they were all in one place. This allowed people to easily be apart of several communities at once. Interestingly enough, most of the people involved were making something! Some were making comedy, some were making music, some were making total, awesome nonsense, but they were all in the same place.

For another year or so, I was able to make music with other people that I'd never met in person. I contributed to VideoSongs with people from all over the globe. If you want to see a crazy amalgamation of talent, tell twenty musicians from around the world to play the same song, then put it all together into one track. It's truly amazing.

During that time, there was a boom of musicians, collaborating and producing music but to be honest, I think we all got tired at the same time, and a huge portion of us just stopped. We saw the limits of the medium, and the lack of financial return from our efforts. For me, at least, the lack of produced income was enough for me to not be able to justify the effort and time that I was putting into it. With a young family waiting for me, I needed to be able to justify my time away. YouTube as a music platform just didn't do it, even with the appearance of things like Patreon (from Jack Conte, no less) and Subbable. I slowly let it go, and fell back into going straight from the office to the dinner table.

I GOT ANTSY AGAIN, but in a different way this time. I was spending more and more time sitting at my computer, writing code for products that didn't really have anything to do with my interests. I started looking for things to do offline, with my hands. I hadn't had a workshop in 3 or 4 years and hadn't gotten to spend much of my time making anything for a really long time.

On occasion, I made things around the house like an aquarium stand and a swing set for my kids. I started thinking of all of things I could make to actually improve our house. At some point, I made a conscious decision to get back into building things. I decided that if I were going to start making things again, I needed to be able to justify the time. I didn't expect that justification to be financial, but there had to be some sort of value in it, which took me back to teaching.

WITH THE POPULARITY of blogs at the time, I realized that doing a how-to blog, would be technically simple for me, and passing on the knowledge, process and mistakes that I made would add value to someone, somewhere (hopefully). I'd had a personal website/blog (now iliketomakestuff.com) for a REALLY long time, but it'd always just been a place for me to brain dump about what I was interested in. There was no topic, or consistency. I decided to start building a focus for the blog and enlisted a good friend of mine, Jonathan, to help me with the look and feel of things. We worked for a couple of months on a logo for I Like To Make Stuff while I started making a few small projects here and there. I took photos along the way, and eventually made posts that consisted of edited photos, and lengthy descriptions of how I made the item.

The first thing I remember making with the express intent to document it, was a coat rack from 2x2, made from plans that I found on Ana White's website (ana-white.com). It wasn't my design, and I was really open about that fact. I wasn't interested in showing off my design skills. I found a plan for something that I needed in my house, and I spent my time trying to explain to others how I went about creating a physical object from a digital plan that I found on the internet.

Immediately, I had friends asking me to make the coat rack for them...for MONEY! I didn't really expect that beforehand, but all of the sudden I was getting orders from people. I started coming up with other ideas of things that I could make, explain online, and eventually sell. In the moment, this seemed like a really good process. In actuality, it wasn't what I wanted to do... not exactly.

I tried my hand at making a bunch of things ahead of time, hoping to sell them to handmade stores and at craft shows, but I ran into a couple of problems right off the bat. First, they didn't sell. I walked away from my first few hand-made shows with barely enough money to cover the gas to get there. Second, I found that replicating one object, several times, ate up all of the time that I was wanting to put into creating stuff for my blog. I quickly got to a point where I needed to decide what my product was. Was it the physical thing I was making? Was it the process, details and explanation?

I knew pretty quickly that I enjoyed the teaching aspect of it way more than the sales end of things. (During my years in the web marketing industry, I realized that I hated being marketed to, and I didn't want to try to convince people to buy what I was creating.) Making that distinction was a pretty key moment for me personally. I realized that marketing was something I wanted very little to do with. A good product, should market itself through it's value. So I decided to focus on providing value. I decided to focus on the blog, and maybe sell the items that were generated through it, on a commission basis. Unfortunately, I immediately ran into another problem. I really didn't enjoy having to figure out how to write down every step of building a project in a way that people could understand. It felt tedious and like a huge amount of extra work after having already made the item.

While I'd been building my blog and creating content, I was still a YouTube user, watching my old musician friends and some consistently funny comedy channels (namely Wheezy Waiter and Rhett and Link). One day I ran across a video by Jimmy Diresta, whom I recognized from his television shows. My wife and I had always watched HGTV and DIY Network. We'd seen Jimmy and his brother in multiple shows, and I knew him as the brother who actually made stuff.

I went down the YouTube rabbit hole, as people often do, finding video after video...creator after creator...genre after genre. Before I knew it, I realized that video was quite possibly the perfect medium for teaching people how to make things. (You would think, after all of that HGTV and DIY Network, it would have been obvious to me.) I watched Jimmy's video, one after the other, blown away at how he made all kinds of different things out of all kinds of different things. I showed my friends his videos, over and over.

I loved seeing Jimmy work at a fast pace. That kept me interested and attentive. I also loved seeing the final product of the video, but I always wanted to know details that he didn't provide (his project videos don't normally include any talking). I wanted to know what a tool was called, or what type of liquid he used to blacken steel, or why he cut something with this saw instead of that one. Out of the format that Jimmy used, came the format that I would eventually use...

- Make it fast.
- Show every single step.
- Explain it in the most concise way I possibly could.
- Demystify the process.

I REALIZED THAT I ALREADY, for the most part, had the technical skills to pull it off a half decent video. I had lots of ideas for how video could be used to teach and explain how things went together. I already had a brand that I'd been building on my blog, and most importantly, I wouldn't have to write as much. I started filming my projects, and piecing together edits, adding voiceover to explain the details of what I was doing and why.

> Side note: I do a 95% complete video edit, cutting out every bit of unnecessary footage while keeping in every step, then I add the voiceover. Speaking to match a tight, lean edit forces me to come up with the most concise way to say things so that it fits within the visual edit.

Over the next year and a half, I made videos every

couple of weeks, as I could fit it into my schedule. I worked a full day at my desk, then spent extra time building or designing a project. Saturday afternoons often included a couple hours of me building in the driveway. My wife was (and still is) very supportive in allowing me extra time to put towards my outside interests. She always allowed me time to play music, train for marathons, make stuff, edit videos, etc. Have I mentioned that she's pretty great? She is.

I made projects videos, posting them to my channel and it grew slowly at first. I found woodworking and maker channels who were doing similar, but different things, and saw another of the YouTube communities pop up that I didn't expect. One of the channels that seemed to pull the community together into one place was The Drunken Woodworker (now called Make Something). David Picciuto created a show that showed off his favorite woodworking videos from the previous week. It was a launching pad for me to learn of new channels and content creators every week. At the end of his shows, he mentioned sending him your videos so he could check them out and maybe feature them. So, I did.

Here's the email I sent David:

"Hey David,

I just wanted to drop you a note to say that I really enjoy the show! Keep it up!

And please give Chuck a raise, he's doing a fantastic job :)

I don't know if my stuff is the type of thing that you'd show, not all of it is woodworking, so I'm not asking you to show any of it, but I thought that you still might find it interesting. Since you asked people to send stuff in, I figured I would. Some of it is just wood, some of it involves other medium. Like you, I'm a software/web guy, so my interests reach outside of woodworking pretty often.

I've got blog posts at iLikeToMakeStuff.com and a channel of videos at http://www.youtube.com/iliketomakestuffcom

Anyway, keep it up, I always look forward to your show..

Bob"

The next week, David showed one of my videos on his show and I watched my subscriber count go from tens to hundreds to thousands. I want to point that out as a mark in time for my business growth. It was something that was almost entirely out of my control but was the first sign of growth I'd seen.

Don't be afraid to take advantage of an opportunity to put yourself out there. I'm NOT saying to send me or anyone specifically your videos in hopes that they'll promote it, but if someone asks, share your work. Online, there's a very fine line between reasonable self promotion and begging. Asking for others to shout you out or promote you will most likely do nothing at all for you. Like I mentioned about marketing, let the product market itself by adding value.

Self promotion and gaining initial traction is one of the hardest parts for most people when it comes to an online presence. Of course, you have to market yourself and your work to a degree, but I'm a firm believer in letting your work speak for itself, and in trying to be the most helpful person in the room. If you bring value with you, you become valuable.

I made more videos, grew a larger subscriber base, and finally started to make a (very) little bit of money from Patreon. Eventually, I turned on ads to my videos which helped a little as well. I started doing a live show, featuring other content creators called BrainPick. It was a chance for me to take questions from a live audience and use those questions to interview other content creators. It worked to cross promote between our channels as well as give the guest creators a different environment to interact with their audience. It was also exhausting and frustrating to try to read questions in real time and act as a host of a show. I diversified my videos to include a series called Maker101, which was kind of a class in tool/technique fundamentals. I tried as hard as I could to maintain consistency in the visual look and feel of what I posted. I tried to be very deliberate about what I did and how I did it. I saw the subscriber count grow and grow.

Side note: Consistency seems to be a theme that always turns up when talking about growth. Releasing consistent content is a way to keep yourself present in the mind of viewers. It creates a pattern, and regardless of what anyone might say, we are drawn to patterns and reliability. Consistency in branding is also massively important, in my opinion. It's important that people recognize your content at first glance. The current state of online media is that there is a HUGE number of platforms for publishing and social media. Having a consistent name, icon and

general presence across platforms will make you
memorable to potential, or even repeat, viewers.

Eventually I got a few small sponsors, which kind of blew me away. People actually wanted to give me money to just mention their products! It allowed me to cover the cost of new tools and materials for projects. (We'll talk a bit more about sponsors later on.)

At that point, I was basically doing two jobs. Well... three. I had my full time software job, my nights and weekends hobby and a family that needed and fully deserved my attention. I needed the day job, I wanted the hobby, and my family wanted and needed me. It was pretty exhausting. Throw in my yearly 18 week, 4 day a week marathon training and all bets were off. I was worn out. My day job was becoming more and more unfulfilling, and I watched several groups of friends get laid off, not knowing how long I'd be worth keeping on the payroll. In my mind, the job was just time that I couldn't put towards my hobby.. this growing, exciting thing that took over more and more of my thoughts and energy. Something had to give.

WHEN A FRIEND FORCES YOU TO
SAY THINGS OUT LOUD

I've got some amazing friends.. lots of them. One of them, in particular, is a guy named Josh. He is one of the more fascinating people you'll ever meet and he has a really amazing talent of untangling things that are confusing and difficult, whether that's in a single person or a group of people. He was constantly encouraging me in my new hobby and always joked (but wasn't joking) about how long before I would do it as my full time job. Josh and I had several conversations where I said things like "I don't want to do software anymore, I want to make content.. but I can't. There's not enough money.. there's this reason and that, and these and ahhhhh.. it's too much to think through!!!!"

Eventually, Josh and his wife, sat down at my dining room table with myself, my wife and a sheet of paper.

He asked me what was standing in my way. He asked me "why can't you do this full time?" but most importantly, he kept asking.. "anything else?"

He wrote it all down, on one sheet of paper. When I couldn't come up with any more reasons not to pursue it, he turned the paper around and said, "so how are you going to overcome these things?"

Josh is really good at forcing me to brain dump all of the stuff that I let cycle in my head. My mind says "I can't do A until I can do B, but B won't work because I need to do C, which can't happen until A is finished....." Each of those things just get in the way of me being able to effective think through and solve the other things, so I just spin. On more than one occasion, Josh has made me say everything out loud, written it down in a way that let's me think through it and actually make sense of it. Everybody needs a Josh.. find yourself a Josh.

By that, I mean, find yourself someone close to you that you trust. Everyone needs a mentor and close friend who can give them an outside perspective. We often get stuck looking at what immediately surrounds us, without being able to see the solutions right out of view. The tendency here might be to reach out and try to find a Josh that is someone you want to emulate, or someone who has experienced what you're going through but I don't think that's necessarily the best. Find someone who has your best interest at heart, and someone who's willing to help you think through tough stuff.

Anyway, after I saw the list of reasons why I was scared to quit my job, it wasn't quite as scary as I'd thought. It became a todo list. By far, the largest item on that list was savings. With a family, security often looks like "having enough money for food and a place to live" so that was the biggest priority. Even as my income from I Like To Make Stuff was increasing, it still wasn't close to what my day job provided, so we planned out a goal of having 3-6 months of living expenses, saved up as a buffer. In all honesty, 6-9 months would have been a smarter goal...I was just impatient.

SOME TIME BEFORE THIS, my wife and I had gone through the Financial Peace University program by Dave Ramsey. Part of this program is geared toward giving you a different perspective on money, specifically debt and savings. It's got some really practical exercises to help you remove debt and increase your savings, both of which are just steps to removing fear and weight from your life. Although I'm not sure where paying off all of our debt fits in this timeline, I can confidently say that it was an absolutely essential part of me being able to attempt to have ILTMS as my full time job. Removing debt isn't essential to everyone's story, but for me, debt has always been a backpack of rocks, making EVERYTHING harder. Debt has stopped me from being able to experience several things in life and once we paid it all off, I felt free. Not only did I not feel like I owed anyone money, but I also had fewer bills to pay every month. Starting your own business is a risk, plain and simple. By removing the liability of debt and building in a savings safety net, you dramatically reduce that risk. I promise it makes a difference in how much focus you can put into your new endeavour. In short, I was concerned with paying for food and a house, not food, house, car payments, credit card bills, loans, etc.

SPRINT TO THE FINISH

Thanks to the prodding of Josh, and many other friends, my wife and I knew what was next. It was time to chase the dream of full time. We talked through the mechanics of it over and over. We both knew that I had to sprint on the work, to create as much as possible, to put as many things in place as I could. I needed to have the momentum in place, so that I could confidently quit the 9-5 when the time came. We decided to put a limit on it though.

When you hear stories of startups or young companies, you often hear about the founders working insane hours, spending every last cent and doing anything it takes to get their idea off the ground. This is common, and in some cases necessary but it's also not sustainable, especially not with a family. I knew that, for a short period of time, I was going to have to buckle down, and do AS MUCH AS POSSIBLE to ramp up ILTMS. I also knew that in that time period, some things were probably not going to get the attention they deserve, namely my relationships and my kids. Here's the thing that I think is really important about this: I made a decision to put a limit on that "sprint" period. The limit wasn't "until I get there" though. That could last for years or never even happen. The limit was a specific time period.

I BELIEVE we set nine months as our evaluation period. At that point, we'd have to take a look at the state of ILTMS vs the 9-5 and see which was working and which was breaking down. The good one would continue on, and the bad one would have to change. So I sprinted, working every free moment on one job or the other. I found myself worrying constantly about if it would work, and what it would mean for our family if it didn't. I was excited about the prospect and the progress but still anxious about the unknown. What if it didn't make enough money? What if we got behind on bills? My wife would pretty regularly say things like "we can eat rice and beans more". She even started looking for a part time job without telling me to be able to bring in supplemental income. I did mention that she's awesome, right?

One evening in particular, I was talking to her about my fear of it not working or not bringing in enough money and she said, "if it doesn't bring in enough, then you get another software job."

Oh... duh. I was so focused on making it work that I'd almost forgotten that I had enough of a skillset that I could fall back into several different trades. It's important to remember that if your YouTube channel about building houses doesn't take off, you can GO BUILD HOUSES.

Side note: I now host a podcast called Making It with Jimmy Diresta and David Picciuto. Several times on the podcast, Jimmy has brought up the saying "What if everything goes right?" It's such a simple thought but a completely different approach to thinking through a risk. Personally, I have a tendency to look at the worst possible outcome as the most likely negative outcome. If you think about it, that's kind of ridiculous. Even if things don't go perfectly, they probably won't go as bad as they possibly can. It'll probably be somewhere in the middle. That makes the outlook not as bad but even better than that is to think through a situation as if everything goes right! Blind optimism is as dangerous as blind pessimism but balance requires looking at both.

THIS CONVERSATION WAS another of those break-through moments like I'd had with Josh. With some realistic encouragement, my wife has destroyed the fear I'd been cycling on for months. Having that fear gone (well, almost gone) made the next few months much easier and more productive.

FROM SPRINT TO DISTANCE PACE

When you run a short race, you can sprint for some or all of it. When you run a distance race, you have to keep your speed in check to make sure that you've got enough strength and stamina to last you until the finish line. When we reached the end of the sprint period, it was completely obvious to my wife, myself and all of those close to me that the 9-5 job had to go. The time and effort I'd put into creating content over those nine months helped the subscriber base and community continue to grow by a huge amount. The momentum was great and the opportunities were becoming greater. I'd received more and more companies interested in sponsoring my videos than I ever expected.

I quit. May 1, 2015 was my last day working in software development. A few weeks before, I'd talked to my manager, who was always very supportive and encouraging about my "hobby". He wasn't surprised at all when I told him that I was going to pursue ILTMS full time. In fact, months before he'd mentioned seeing some of my videos and said that my calling wasn't in software, it was as a producer.

That was an encouraging and terrifying thing to hear in a one on one call with my manager. It sounded like the beginning of a conversation where I was about to be let go but he was just being encouraging. He was super supportive of my going after this new direction.

ON MY FIRST day of full time, I took my camera into my back yard and made a video telling my viewers that I'd made the jump. Mostly I wanted to thank them for making it a possibility. The comments on that video are still some of the nicest, most encouraging ones on any of my videos.

https://www.youtube.com/watch?v=iwxpRhn4zuM

PART 2

VULNERABILITY

When something is a hobby, it's kind of inconsequential. If someone tells you you're not good at golf, it's not the end of the world. If you're a professional public speaker and some one tells you that you have an awful voice, that IS kind of a big deal. Maybe that's a condition of us wrapping our identity around our careers (that's probably a whole different book) but it still hurts when someone tells you that you're not good at something that is really important to you. Now imagine that you walked away from a well paying, stable job to do something you love. Also imagine that every other day, an anonymous person somewhere in the world lobs a hurtful insult at you about how bad you are at your new job. Maybe I've got thin skin, but it hurts. YouTube (and the internet in general) is a minefield for thin skinned creators. Every step can result in an expletive filled rant on why you shouldn't exist, or how you wasted three minutes of their life.

FOR A LONG TIME, this REALLY got to me, even

though other creators would say, *"just let the bad comments go", "you've just got to ignore them"*. I put my time and effort into making something that I thought had value, then I GAVE it away. Even small attacks seemed personal. I could try to be objective and think "this is probably a rude pre-teen hiding behind their parents computer. They probably feel bad about themselves and are taking it out on me." Even if that was true, it still got to me and the comments would stick with me, sometimes for a couple of days after I deleted them. Early on, they just made me feel gross. They stole my motivation to be productive. On a couple of occasions, I did think "if I'm going to feel this way after every video because of one random jerk, I don't want to do this anymore." After all, no one ever insulted me in my coding team meetings.

THOUGHTS like that made me realize how I was allowing something external, in the form of a faceless YouTube comment, to affect the positive effect I could have on literally hundreds of thousands of people. While I learned to internally deal with negative comments, I noticed a lot of things about how people communicate and why they say what they say. I also started to understand that people ingest media for many different reasons. This was really important as I figured out what my response to this negativity was going to be. I figured that I had a few options. I could respond in the same mean, angry voice. I could apologize or publicly take offense. I could try to reason with them and plead my case. Ultimately, I decided on my blanket response to negative, hurtful comments: **delete them and move on**.

There are two main reasons why this is the way I

decided to handle them. The biggest reason is that since I'm in control of who and what can be allowed to stay in my comments section, I have the opportunity to shape the community around my content. For me, having a community that is inviting and positive is hugely important to my goal of motivating and inspiring people. I mean, no one will ask questions about things they want to learn if they're worried about being made fun of or attacked. By deleting abusive comments and blocking aggressive users, the voices that are heard are the uplifting and encouraging ones. The purpose is NOT to create an echo chamber of "pro-Bob" voices. I don't block people who disagree with me or think different. I block users (and remove comments) that are abusive.

I BEGAN to look for ways to gain some perspective on these negative comments and negative people in general. One day, I saw a comment that said something to the effect of *"Why don't you do _____ anymore? That's why I subscribed to your channel. I'm unsubscribing."* That comment gave me a huge insight to the relationship of creator and consumer. The insight was all about expectations.

EXPECTATIONS

When I go to a Mexican restaurant, I expect there to be Mexican food on the menu. If the menu is all Asian food, I'll probably complain because it's not what I expected. If I go to a cafeteria style restaurant, the expectation is that the available options are always different and not one particular type of cuisine. The people who run those restaurants have zero control over what I expect to see on the menus, and they also don't have any reason to adjust their menu to accommodate one person's expectations.

I realized that I could respond to a comment like the one above in a couple of ways. I could adjust my content to try to make that person happy, but that will just make me not meet the expectations of someone else.

I could respond in kind "Fine, unsubscribe. I don't like your attitude" and look like a total jerk who got his feelings hurt. Or, I could completely ignore it and realize that every time a person like that unsubscribes, the more reasonable my subscriber base gets. That's one less person who isn't fully on board with what I'm doing.

Someone asked me once how to build a subscriber base.

I said to just do what ONLY YOU can do, and the audience will find you because they love that thing. It dawned on me that I should be taking my own advice in regards to comments. The more passionately and purely I chased what I wanted to create, what ONLY I could create, the more dedicated the subscribers would become. The ones who weren't interested would move on, which was perfectly fine. Ten people who fully support you is infinitely more valuable than hundreds who are mildly interested.

My internal response to negative comments has matured a lot over the past year, and hopefully will continue to do so. Realizing that I have no responsibility to meet everyone's expectations removed a lot of the pressure and helped me not take those comments personally. To anyone who creates anything, and deals with that negativity, it does get easier (in the form of you not caring as much), I promise.

(To be fair, in my case, the negative and mean comments are 1 in 1000. The VAST majority of comments directed towards me online are helpful, encouraging and supportive. Those are the ones that matter, and the ones that I still remember to this day.)

PRO TIP: Don't leave someone a comment telling them that you're unsubscribing. It's childish.

OPENING UP

Being vulnerable and transparent in your creations gives outsiders a more pure view into who you are. It also gives the bad guys a line of sight to your weakest parts. Just like in a relationship, there's always some risk in being vulnerable. The more you're willing to expose, the closer you'll become to those that you let in. In my opinion, that's how close communities form. You can choose any amount of involvement when interacting with your supporters but let me tell you that a close knit community of dedicated supporters is worth the risk of a gut punch from a stranger.

Never in my wildest dreams did I expect my silly videos about making things to have life changing effects anywhere. Contrary to my expectations (I'm fully aware of the irony regarding "expectations") I've seen deep friendships form and lives literally changed and saved because I was willing to share who I was both in videos and on social media. (I'll talk more about this later when I cover impact.)

SHARING

Part of getting your creations in front of other people is taking advantage of the existing social networks. It's the modern equivalent of hanging a flyer for your band's show up in a busy mall (kind of). Social networks are where the people are, and where they share what they like with their friends. They're a useful, and almost necessary, tool in our tech landscape for distributing self published content.

I've tried, since the beginning of ILTMS to be very engaged in current social media (as of mid 2016, that means Instagram, Facebook, Twitter, Snapchat, Periscope). This has been a double edged sword, with the positive side being the sharpest. Content production is generally a kind of broadcast. You create something, push it into the world, then observe the response at a distance. For me, social media has been how I follow up and engage in personal conversations in regards to my creations, but also just on a personal level. Some creators use the networks purely as a marketing tool, relaying links to their content for maximum exposure. That is helpful, but I've found that personal interactions and response help build that community of dedicated supporters in a way that the broadcast approach probably can't. I've learned a lot about the individuals who watch my videos and listen to my podcasts. I know so many of these people by name and like old friends, it's nice to see messages pop up from them on occasion.

The downside to this type of more ground level interaction is that it's growth mostly follows the growth of your community at large. Actually that's not a downside, but maintaining the same level of interaction is tough when you go from 200 to 20,000 Twitter followers. As your networks grow, even if you're only focusing on one, it gets harder to maintain the same personal feel. I've personally felt the urge to back off of that personal interaction, and probably have to a small degree over this first year. Ultimately, I think it's truly important to stay connected to the people who support you, in any way, shape or form.

Another use for social media, maybe more so for the general population, is as a way to spread person things to those close to you. Kid photos, family events, etc all end up in Facebook albums so that your family and friends can see them. But what about the networks that don't account for a personal/professional distinction (most of them)? I certainly wasn't interested in creating and maintaining two profiles on every network to use in different ways.

I found myself in a strange place. I wanted to share, but also had to figure out where the limit was of what's relevant, and safe.

I decided pretty early on that I wanted everything I do to be built around who I am, all of me, not just a cherry picked part of me that is publicly acceptable. That doesn't mean that I share every single thing I do, but I want to be identified as a husband, a father, a runner, a musician, etc as well as a maker and content creator.

One time on Instagram, I posted a couple photos of my kids in succession and someone commented "looks like it's time for a separate family Instagram account". My response was as much for me as it was him. "Maybe you have the wrong idea of what my Instagram is :)" I realized that outside expectations of what my social media looked like may get a little bruised if I continued to mix professional and personal posts. Conversely, including my family and real life experiences along side my projects connected me to a lot of my supporters in a very real, personal way.

MY POINT in all of this is that social media will grow with you, but as it grows, there are pains. Find a way to use it for marketing, but also (and maybe more importantly) as a community building tool. It can easily become something that eats up a large amount of your time, so keep it in check. If it gets in the way of your productivity, then it may not be helping you as much as you think. Since I mentioned productivity...

BEING PRODUCTIVE

I'm wired differently than some, I realize this. When looking back through my life, I can see so many signs of the things I realize about myself now. For example, every time I changed or fixed something growing up, I took photos before I made any change. I'd take a few photos along the way, but mostly just when it was completed. I used to keep track of books that I read or how many consecutive comic books I had. Remember the backs of Star Wars action figures with the rows of every figure available? Yeah, I checked those off to keep track of my entire collection. One of my favorite projects at my old job was building a data visualization library, a way to visually quantify what we knew based on the information we had.

I like to measure change over time. I like to see proof of progress. I can see now that I'm drawn to things that make it easier to gauge that progress. For example, a video that shows every single change from raw materials to finished product. This helps a lot with being productive. How do you know if you're being productive if you don't measure a change over time?

OVER MY FIRST YEAR, I've adjusted both my means of measuring progress and my means of doing the work. I think these will continue to change as I grow into new areas and have more and different things to measure. Up to this point, a big part of measuring was having a schedule. If I set a due date for project X, it was easy to tell if I met or missed that date. If there was no due date, then there's no such thing as "late" and that will most definitely effect whatever I want to do after project X. Scheduling is a huge part of project management in any situation and also one of the most common things I hear from people who produce great content. They often say "no matter what the timeframe is, release content on a schedule. People know when to expect it and look forward to it." I would totally agree with that "release" schedule, but it's potentially different than a "production" schedule.

I nailed down a release schedule pretty early on although I never exposed that schedule publicly online. Releasing videos every two weeks while I was working a 9-5 was the best I could do, but when I jumped to full time, that simply was not enough content to make it work. Part of my pre full time sprint was adjusting to releasing videos once a week. Now that I think about it, I don't know if subscribers even noticed that. I don't remember ever getting comments about increased release frequency.

Regardless, I picked a weekly release day, Thursday. There's no magic in the day choice though. I simply looked at a bunch of channels in my genre and found that there were fewer releases on that day than any other. This meant that the viewer would potentially have fewer options to watch on that day, and my video might have a better chance of getting seen. I honestly have no way of telling if that actually mattered at all.

ONCE I PICKED that release day, I reverse engineered a production schedule. For me, I knew that my Patreon supporters needed to see the video at least one day early, which meant the video actually needed to be complete by Wednesday. I continued to work backwards. Voiceover, graphics, final edit, rough edit, shooting, material gathering, project design, etc. Of course, depending on the project, those steps can have very different time lines, or be totally non-existent. The main exercise was finding points through out the week to gauge productivity. If the shooting was completed Monday night, I could edit and voiceover Tuesday to release privately on Wednesday, then publicly on Thursday. Having a loose timeline like that made a HUGE difference in planning multiple videos and figuring out their production overlap.

One of the ongoing issues with consistent production is that overlap. If every project could be done start to finish in one week, it'd be easy. What about the big projects that take multiple weeks? What about realizing mid way through shooting that you're missing a key material and it's sold out? There are a million ways that a tight timeline can get out of whack. To build in a buffer for those issues that disrupt schedules, you have to get ahead, and that is tough. This is admittedly something that I'm still not great at. I go through times where I have a two or even three week buffer of content, but life often takes advantage of that buffer and it gets used up. This is similar in principle and practice to the financial buffer we put in place before quitting the 9-5.

Both of these are there for a reason. They get used, then rebuilt over time.

I'm finding, a good way to build that schedule buffer is to plan out multiple small projects that you can shoot all at once, or at least in succession. Batch processing anything helps make it more productive. Deciding to spend two straight days shooting builds makes that time more productive than splitting those three shoots up over three weeks. The shop is in production mode with lights and cameras setup and ready to use for as long as it takes to produce those three videos. Then, the whole focus turns to editing, then voiceover, etc.

BOTH TIM FERRISS AND MERLIN MANN (podcasters that I enjoy) talk about the cost of task switching and how it affects productivity. For example, I only ever make any progress on this book when I'm on a plane or waiting in an airport. Those are times where I don't have many other distractions and interruptions. I can write something semi cohesive because there's nothing breaking up my flow and attention. At home, everything in my office and shop, my kids, the dogs, laundry.. all of it would be vying for my attention and I might be able to write for 10 minutes here and there. Trust me, it would make less sense than it does now.

Tim and Merlin both talk about the "cost of task switching". Essentially, your brain has to re-adjust when you switch tasks. If you're writing an email and you hear a loud noise, there's a moment of confusion while your brain reorients to the new thing to focus on. This is natural and only takes a second or two, but the fewer transitions in your day, the fewer re-adjustments are necessary. You lose less time when you batch process things.

The point being, batch process the different pieces of production where you can. The time will be more productive and you'll have three things in progress, rather than one thing complete. Also, having multiple projects open at any time gives you a productivity fallback. If project A gets stuck, go be productive on project B.

The idea of batching for productivity runs into all sorts of things. I do my best (but still fail miserably) to NOT check social media every ten minutes throughout the day. I find it's better for my productivity to spend ten minutes on it in the morning, then at mid day, then at night. That's regular enough to keep me in touch without being too focused on replies and feed browsing. The same goes for email. I used to try to respond to contact and business emails within 24 hours, but now I focus on business emails first, then general contact emails once or twice a week. I sit down on the couch after the kids go to bed, once a week and respond to 20-30 emails in a big group. (The doesn't keep me current, but does keep the email response flow moving so they don't sit indefinitely).

FILLER OR EXPANSION

Another way I've tried to maintain or augment my production schedule while maintaining my release schedule is adding different types of content. I had a few other types of video series that I'd wanted to make and they had a very different (generally smaller) production requirement. Throwing in these easier to produce shows occasionally, I was able to add to that buffer and still be producing content for the regular schedule.

But is it just filler? Well, hopefully not. The idea is not to create junk content to hit a release date, but to find a different format that both provides value and is easier to produce. The value doesn't necessarily have to be the same as the core content (in my case, project videos) but if it's empty filler, people will notice and they won't watch it. In that case, you're actually making it worse for yourself.

Expanding your type of content is another place where some consumers will probably grumble because they weren't expecting it, but any change you make (and stick with) will become the new normal after a short while.

I've added multiple types of shows over my first year.

They're never as popular as my core content type, but they have served purposes both for the viewers and for me. I've got plans along these same lines for year two but instead of adding to the buffer, the shorter, simpler shows will double the content output. We'll see how that goes, but as long as the production impact is relatively low and they have value, I think they'll be a worthwhile addition.

Even if the schedule runs smoothly, producing anything on a regular and extended basis can be exhausting. Eventually, you may have to change directions to save your sanity.

PIVOT

Sometimes, you get burnt out or things simply don't turn out to be what you had imagined. As much as I think consistency is great, sometimes you just have to change. Personally, I haven't really had to do this in a big public way, but I've had several internal pivots over my first year of full time.

For me, one good example is my show BrainPick. This started as a live video interview show where I was the host and I handled choosing and asking questions, to the guest, that had been submitted from the live audience. This format was pretty great in a lot of ways, and people really enjoyed it. Over time, however, I did not. I found that a live show driven by a guest and user submitted questions could be pretty unpredictable. I was stuck trying to keep it all moving along without completely falling apart. My only real purpose in that format was moderating. I loved the idea of talking to these people and learning about how they got to be who they were, but the format was exhausting. So, I changed it.

I'D STARTED A PODCAST, called Making It, during that first year with David Picciuto and Jimmy Diresta. It was conversational, just three different people intersecting at a common passion. The show became such a comfort that I decided to try to carry it's overall feel over to BrainPick and make it a podcast. There was no audience, no live aspect and it worked much better, in my mind. Guests can still be unpredictable, but at least there's editing.

Many other creators have made similar shifts, or even some that were far more dramatic. In a lot of cases, that pivot was driven by a personal change and it was necessary for them to be continue to enjoy what they were doing. Again, those big dramatic changes can be jarring for the audience with whom you've built a certain expectation. Part of that change, as a creator, is being patient while they adjust to the new normal. Plus, if one pivot doesn't work, you can always pivot in a different direction.

My major pivot was leaving software and doing ILTMS full time. Maybe that's not as drastic (externally) as going from comedy to politics, but it was a pivot towards something that I loved more and had potential to make more of a difference.

IMPACT

Don't get me wrong, even mundane, under appreciated jobs can make a HUGE difference. Real change happens at eye level, person to person. That doesn't take a huge platform or lots of resources. However, the impact of my 9-5 was helping a small subset of IT professionals install software on more and more computers at a distance. That's not exactly personal impact. I'm also not going to lie and say that I left that job simply because I wasn't having a personal impact. I left because I wanted to do something more, something that I didn't really expect to have an impact either. At most, I expected to have some weekend warrior DIYers make some stuff to enjoy, or maybe some parents make some projects with their kids.

Well before I even considered doing ILTMS as a career, I had a purpose for it (I'll get to that later). If people got inspired to even try making something they wanted, I would have been happy. I was completely blown away with the emails that began to arrive. As I entered my sprint period, and content increased, I saw more and more messages from people come in.

I got emails from veterans who were lost after they got home, with nothing to occupy their hands and minds. On multiple occasions, they said that my videos (and other creators like me) ignited motivation in them to do something. In some cases, this trickled down to affecting how they dealt with their families. One guy told me that his marriage almost ended until my videos inspired him to make some projects. That interest reconnected he and his wife and saved their marriage! There have been similar stories of vets with no real reason to continue on after they came home, some suicidal. Hearing from a random stranger that your video saved their life will change the way you think about what you do, I can assure you.

I've seen people reach out for counseling help in comments sections, I've heard from teens who decided to go to engineering school instead of skip college altogether, and on and on.

I'm not saying any of this to prove anything about myself, but to show you how something as simple as a project video can literally have a life changing impact on someone you may never meet in person. As you build a platform, you build reach. That reach is both arms and fingers. By that, I mean that the arms of your reach go further into the world around more people, but the fingers can go to a personal level and have a specific impact on each one of them. You can motivate and inspire people toward something that they love. This connects back to the social media topic pretty heavily as well. The amount of interaction and the depth of interaction you have with people DOES matter.

THE IMPACT that we have as creators will, more often

than not, be more subtle than some of those emails that I mentioned. It may not even be noticed by the consumers for a long time, if ever. For example, I make a concerted effort to keep my kids in mind when I'm making something. I don't expect my kids to necessarily have interest in making things like I do, or creating content, but how I work has an impact on them. Obviously, it has a direct financial impact on them, but I mean more of a "create vs consume" impact. A subconscious thought like "why buy it if I can make it" can change a person in a lot more ways than teaching them how to make a particular type of joinery. Also, my kids will grow up knowing that their dad left an unfulfilling, but safe job for something that he cared about, and they can do that too.

I can also say, as a creator and consumer, one of the best ways you can encourage someone that you respect and appreciate is to tell them so. More than that, tell them why. Tell them the impact they've had on you.

Hearing how you've impacted someone expands your understanding of what you do. That understanding can inform how to pursue your purpose.

PURPOSE

This is a tricky subject. It's unfair to say that every endeavor needs to have a life changing purpose. I'm not talking about coming up with how you're going to change the world when I talk about purpose. I mean finding the answer to "why?". Why am I interested in this? Why am I willing to risk anything (or everything) for this? That can be a large, complex answer. That can be a one word answer. That can be a complete unknown. Everyone will care differently about defining a purpose for what they do. I can only speak for myself, so let me tell you about my purpose and why I needed to know it.

LIKE I MENTIONED EARLIER, I needed to work with my hands, for my own well being. Also, I felt the need to justify the time I was spending in the shop, away from my family. Turning that time into something outward facing was enough for me to justify it. If my time in the shop can help someone else learn something, then it had value and might be worthwhile. That purpose worked for a long time for me, but as my focus shifted to wanting to do more and more content creation, I found that purpose becoming too vague.

The more I created, the more feedback I got. I had people telling me that they enjoyed how I explained things, and that it simplified what they'd seen elsewhere. The biggest eye opener for me was someone saying that after seeing one of my project videos, they weren't afraid to try a project they'd been avoiding for a long time. That message helped me refine my purpose. As it changed (in my head) I decided that I should probably be a little more explicit about defining my purpose. Eventually, I sat down to write out an informal mission statement for myself. The real reason for this was to record what I thought my purpose was at that point and time. It was changing and I knew it would continue to change. Writing it down gave me a model to work against as I made decisions. I wanted a standard to vet my choices against and I think it made a huge difference.

WE'RE EGOTISTICAL, we're human. My ego can make me think that all sorts of bad ideas are actually good ideas. Having my purpose well defined helps me know if a choice I'm about to make is furthering my purpose or if it's just feeding my ego.

My purpose for ILTMS in it's shortest form:
I want to remove all barriers to entry so people are inspired to make the things that they want to have. To remind them that they are capable of more than they think.

I decided that I wanted to spend my time on things that I, personally, wanted to make. Most of it was based on a need I saw. Some of it was for friends, some of it was just interesting. But, those objects were not the goal.

Through making these projects, I had the chance to do two major things, and these became really important.

1. By showing every single step of a process, the viewer ended the video with no unknowns. They may not have been able to accomplish all of those steps (yet) but they could see that there was no magic in making that project. It was just a series of small steps to get to the final objective.

2. I always say that a big problem is really just a collection a small problems. I have the chance to show how solving small problems can fix the big one. This is something that can go WAY past making physical things in someone's life. The process for making a box is kind of sequential. It's a process that builds on the previous step. Preparing for college is the same thing. Studying => good tests => college => wage => food, etc.

Both of these are valuable by themselves, but the real culmination of them, to me, is seeing someone use those two things to go attempt something that THEY care about, make something THEY want to have.

I realize that there's a small percentage of people who want to make a project that I show in one of my videos, but that direct instruction is not the point of the videos.

This is reinforced for me in how I see myself respond to different interactions. Recently at a conference, someone said "I love your videos!" and I felt good and it was nice. I passed someone on the escalator who yelled "I bought power tools because of you!" and I felt incredible. He didn't just like my content. He took an action.. a step towards something for himself.

But that's MY purpose, not yours. It shouldn't be yours, because you're not me. You should find your own through trial and error and feedback and failure. The purpose doesn't have to be humanitarian or altruistic. It can be as simple as "I love music, I want to express what I'm going through". The point I want you to think about is that by defining a purpose for what you're doing, you set up a gauge for yourself. This gauge helps you know how well you're doing, how close you're sticking to what you set out to do.

It can help keep you on track, and give you some validation when you see evidence of that purpose being played out in what you do.

On the other hand, I have friends who change the "why" of what they do all of the time. Their purpose isn't as clear cut, or at least as stationary. Today it's "have fun!", tomorrow it's "become great at ___", next it's "learn to ___". I think the purpose can change like each of us do. In that case, if you can't settle on a purpose, maybe you need to zoom out. Maybe your purpose isn't any of those things specifically. Maybe it's "explore something new every day". Something more general like that covers those different interests, but still works as a gauge for making choices. If you're having trouble finding your "why" and defining your purpose, zoom out or maybe zoom in. Change your perspective and see if that helps you get a better view and ultimately define it.

To be fair, I've spent a LOT of time thinking about this. It's not an afternoon long process (or maybe it will be for you). You'll find it if you look for it, and it will probably continue to evolve over time. For me, it also helps me know when my job is finished, where my responsibility ends.

RESPONSIBILITY

I have lots of responsibilities. Most of us do. I'm responsible for providing for my family. My role there is really clear. I may not know HOW to be the father, husband and provider that I should be, but I know WHAT needs to be done. In a corporate job, we usually know what we're responsible for (if we have a good boss). It's clear cut when we can submit the report and walk away. Creating content can be far more confusing in regards to responsibility.

As a creator, am I responsible for making everyone happy? Am I responsible to fully explain everything at a college level detail? Am I responsible for evenly speaking to different demographics? It goes on and on. I've gone around and around trying to figure out how responsible I am for the safety of the people who use tools because they saw me use them.

There IS a lot of responsibility with teaching or inspiring people, but I'm not bound to cover and be responsible for everything. Defining my purpose helped me figure some of that out as well.

Case in point, viewers constantly ask me to do videos

only using hand tools because that's all they have access to. If my purpose was to create globally accessible wood-working videos, then yes, I should make hand tool videos. I should also make some only using a knife, or maybe only using fallen trees, etc. I can completely appreciate the request. I get it, but that's not my purpose. Defining my purpose helps me internally say "No. That's not a necessary part of accomplishing what I've set out to do." It's certainly one possible way to accomplish my purpose, but I'm not responsible for accommodating people in that situation.

Listening to some online educators recently, I realized how they also struggle with the responsibility to validate the information that they teach. It's very easy to redistribute false information even with the best of intentions. In this digital world, once content is released it's extremely hard to update and correct it. Luckily these educators have defined what they are actually responsible for and take it very seriously.

For me, my responsibility to the viewer also has another tricky thing that I have yet to figure out. The crux of it is that I intentionally do things, pretty often, for the very first time, on camera. This means that I, pretty often, do things very wrong. When I learn a new skill, just like anyone else, I don't know the best practices, the ins and outs, the correct terminology. The reason I make those videos and leave in my mistakes is to be honest. I'm not a professional. I'm a student. Part of learning is breaking things badly enough that you remember to do it differently next time. The issue of responsibility comes into play here in regards to my content staying online indefinitely.

For example, if I use a new saw, for the first time and make a cut that is not the safest way to do it, I have no way of updating that video to voice a better way. Yes, I can leave comments regarding it (that no one will read).. I can make a follow up video, but without removing that original content, my mistake lives on. I have yet to figure out how responsible I am for the "unanswered" mistakes that I leave online. My hope is to learn from them and the helpful comments, then make improvements next time.

For some context, I still get weekly comments about videos that I made 3 years ago, pointing out my errors. Reliving those mistakes over and over in the comments section is just one of the many things that I absolutely did NOT expect when deciding to go full time.

WHAT I DIDN'T EXPECT

If it's not obvious, I'm a strange mixture of a *pre*crastinator (that's the opposite of a procrastinator) and a somewhat impulsive child. I'm kind of like the person who researches the best type of parachute for months, finds the best deal, repacks the chute 5 times for safety, watches tons of skydiving videos, then decides to go bungee jumping at the last minute.

I know this about myself NOW, but it's a fairly new revelation.

Before I went full time, I planned...a LOT. Most of it was really helpful. I looked at my growth rate on YouTube, all of my different income sources and time investment. Very few things online are predictable, but based on the rate of growth in those things up to that point, I made some plans based on what I expected the first year to look like. (Don't forget, I had a financial buffer just in case things changed).

I projected out how much I was expecting to make over time and how much, if any, my time commitment would have to increase (based the typical 40 hours a week).

The long and short of it... I was wrong.

I was wrong about the growth. It grew exponentially faster than I expected.

I was wrong about the income. It was less consistent month to month, but greater overall than I expected.

Most of all, I was wrong about the time investment.

RECENTLY I SAW a post on Instagram that said something to the effect of "It's FRIDAY!!!! Unless you work for yourself, it's always Wednesday." This perfectly sums it up, in my mind.

Let me be clear here, I think it's REALLY bad for anyone to work every minute of every day. I think it leads to burnout, and will eventually make you dread what used to be your passion. I think balance is WAY more beneficial in more ways than we can know. But with that said, there is ALWAYS work to be done.

I don't think that means that you have to always DO that work, but it's there waiting for you after you go for a walk, when you wake up at 4am, when you get back from the beach.

Even though I have owned businesses before (in fact I've worked for myself more than I've worked for others) I was still completely naive to the fact that there would ALWAYS be work waiting for me to tackle.

I WARNED before about working all of the time, and that is still true, but I also LOVE the fact that there's work to be done, simply because I LOVE the work! For me, the balance to find is about spending time and effort on different things that I love. I love my work. I love my family.

They both need me to do my part for their survival and it's my responsibility to constantly reassess if I'm in balance. Like with the sprint I mentioned earlier, some things are seasonal. Sometimes, my kids need me to be Dad more than usual. Sometimes, work requires me to spend the time preparing to provide for my family. Personally, I don't think balance, in this situation, means a fixed ratio like 40%/60%. I think it's in flux constantly, with the weight shifting where it's needed, when it's needed. It's not "balanced", it's "balancing".

I also did not expect how challenging it would be to keep an idea book full. I have a LOT of ideas, and I drop every single one into a bank to pull from later, (I'll talk more about this in the PROCESS section.) but they're not all good ideas. At the beginning of my full time "journey", I could look at my list of 50+ projects and think "I'll never possibly get through everything. It grows faster than I can check them off!". However, I didn't expect it to be such a challenge to overlap them into a schedule that kept my content varied in type and scope. By that, I mean that I didn't want to only do small woodworking projects that took an afternoon. I also didn't want to only make massive month long builds that span multiple videos. The hard thing, that I still haven't figured out how to deal with, is that my project list is a combination of every type, size, and scope of project. Some of those are great ideas, but just not realistic, at least now. Some are great but too repetitive. Some are great but will take too long. Some are great but require tools that I don't have. Some are, not great.

When you (temporarily) remove those ideas from the list, it gets much smaller. I just wasn't expecting how tough it would be to continually find projects to do, that I could produce as well as stay on my release schedule. I'm still working on this one, to be honest.

I DID NOT EXPECT to get recognized, on occasion, in random places. I'm not saying this to make myself sound famous, or anything to that effect. I honestly did not consider that I might ever be recognizable to anyone outside of the people that I actually know. It doesn't happen often, and when it does, it's mostly great to meet people. There have been a couple of strange interactions but I've been lucky to meet some really fantastic people and get to learn about them.

I'm currently sitting in the food court in the JetBlue terminal at JFK airport writing this. Last year, on this same weekend, in this same airport someone saw me sitting in this same group of tables. They didn't say hello, but instead sent me a message saying that they saw me on my laptop but didn't want to bother me. That was very nice of them, but at the same time, it made me realize that when you put yourself online, a certain group of people will know you, whether you know them or not. It's just another of the things I didn't expect.

I did not expect there to be SO MUCH EMAIL. It's crazy, honestly, but it's also my own fault. In my pursuit of staying connected to my audience, I drove people to the contact page on my website, as a way to get in touch with me. By using that form, I could drive all inquiry through a single funnel, in theory. In reality, this doesn't work for a lot of reasons, namely social media. Regardless of how I try to get people to go through my site, people will always use what is most convenient for them, and that is often Facebook messages (even to my personal account), Twitter or

Instagram direct messages. Setting those aside, I tried to use email as a queue to answer them in the order that I received them.

So, here's why it was bad. Every different type of email was coming into the same queue. I added filters and tags and labels. Then moved business inquiries to a separate inbox, and a separate form on the website. The non-business emails still rolled in and often were asking the same questions. I put a Frequently Asked Questions section above the form on my contact page, theoretically forcing people to look for the answer before emailing me a question. Even still, a lot of the emails are the same questions over and over. The larger problem was the length of some of the messages. I was receiving very long, very heartfelt message that were humbling and amazing sometimes, but they took a long time to read. It took an even longer time to craft a thoughtful response to them.

Eventually, I had put a character limit on the form to trim down the first message in the conversation. I would recommend this for anyone as it keeps the introduction short enough to be able to respond to.

These emails, all of them, are amazing and I'm truly grateful that people want to share with me. I just didn't realize there would be so many. When it comes down to it, those interactions are the fingers of our reach that I mentioned earlier. Those are the messages and moments we get to encourage and uplift someone who has reached out to us. I don't take that lightly, and that's why I do my best to respond to as many as I can, in a thoughtful way.

If you're growing a community, be prepared for this and plan accordingly. If you're a community member and want to encourage someone your respect, remember that they've probably got a lot of input and be patient with them. They won't always be able to help you solve your problems, help you promote your newest creation, or tell you where to go to college.

Things like email, social media, shipping products, editing, website posting, all cost time and that time will add up very quickly. Eventually, I found that those things were adding up for me in a way that wasn't manageable by myself. About six months after going full time, I hired an editor.

GETTING HELP

The prospect of hiring someone to help you is scary. It feels like you're giving up a part of this thing that IS YOU to someone else. In this way, I was really blessed to already have someone that I trusted with this. One of my best friends in the world, Jonathan, also happens to have been a past employee, fellow band member, lived in my spare room for a couple of months and designed my logo and branding for ILTMS. Basically, he's part of the family. He's a freelance graphic designer and has always done design work for me to help keep ILTMS moving. When I needed more help with video editing, he stepped right in without any prior experience. That may seem like a good reason NOT to hire someone, but it worked out great. Essentially, he watched me edit one of the videos, then took the next one on his own. I spent some time changing his edit to match previous videos as far as pace and timing and showed him what had changed. The very next video was entirely his edit, and he's been doing them ever since. That's been over a year and a half at this point.

The reason I wanted to voice all of that is that it can be

daunting to try to hire someone with a very specific skillset, but what may work better in the long run is to look for someone around you that you trust (remember Josh?). If you have a good relationship with someone who's interested and teachable, you can teach them how to help you. The same applies to things like website postings, and even general social media management. Anyone with basic computer skills can handle posting new content, but if you get someone you know and trust, you're more likely to bring them closer into your process and will probably find more things that they can help with.

SPEAKING OF PROCESS

Everyone has a different process, or even no process. For me personally, I've put a few things in place to help me track ideas and production schedules, like I've mentioned before. Having these things in some sort of digital tool made it really easy for me to hire someone to take on part of the work. Those tools allow us to collaborate and update each other in ways that a bunch of sticky notes would not.

Depending on when you're reading this, the tools may have changed, but as of this writing, I rely heavily on a few free services, namely Trello and Slack.

Slack is a general chatroom tool, but has lots of integrations with other softwares and that's what makes it really powerful. It's great for group or one on one conversations.

Trello is basically the sticky notes I mentioned before, but in digital form. It's awesome, and general enough that you can use it in lots of different ways.

Those are the specific tools that I use, but there are lots of options and I think what is more important, is HOW I use them.

TRELLO IS where I keep most of my information. For my schedule and ideas, I have multiple "boards". The boards (much like whiteboards on a wall) are named things like "Project Schedule", "Project Ideas", "Sponsorship opportunities" and "New Show Ideas". These are pretty self explanatory, but they're laid out in slightly different ways.

The "Project Schedule" board has a list for each of the next four or five (rolling) months. Each list has a card for each project I plan to release in that month. Each card has all of the information I have for that project. It has reference photos, sketches, links, checklists, sponsorship info and most importantly, a due date.

At a glance, I can see the state of things. I can see what's coming up soon and what I need to be working on for the coming weeks and months. It even provides a calendar view using those dates to place the cards.

The "Project ideas" board contains a set of lists for me to organize the ideas by plausibility. I've got lists like "Definitely", "Maybe" and "Totally Bananas". That last one is for ideas that likely won't ever happen, but are too good to throw away. I've also got a list there called "Incoming" where I can quickly drop any new project idea in an instant, without having to worry about categorizing it. Basically, this board is a staging ground for ideas that get moved to the Project Schedule when I'm ready to take them on. The power here is gathering all ideas instantly, and being able to sort them into categories when there's time.

To capture these ideas, I can enter them directly into the website or app, but as usual, I like to complicate things. Most of these modern tools will connect to services like IFTTT (If This, Then ThaT). It's power is being able to take an input from one service and have it trigger something in another service. It allows me to jot down an idea in a fast, simple interface (using the IFTTT app on my phone). It automatically sends that note to Trello, and creates an item in the "Incoming" list of my "Project Ideas" board. It may seems complicated, but a few minutes of setup allows me to record ideas from anywhere quickly, easily and with very little effort. That makes me more likely to do it.

Another heavily used board is one named "Sponsorship Opportunities". It lets me keep track of the state of sponsor negotiations, contracts, etc. which can get completely lost in email chains very, very easily. As long as I keep them filled with relevant information, they also act as a ledger. I keep a history there of when I worked with a sponsor, what we did together, how they behaved, what the terms of the agreement were, how much I made from it, etc. It's great to be able to go back and gather that type of information about ANY past sponsorship deal from a single place.

The point I'm trying to make is that I keep track of a whole lot of different types of things, with just a couple of free tools. You don't necessarily have to invest yourself into a large, expensive project management application just to stay organized.

But I mentioned sponsors, and that's probably something that you're itching to hear about. So, let's get to it.

SPONSORSHIP & INCOME

Money. It's essential and annoying. It's the thing that a lot of us hate to care about. The fact of the matter is that any career, no matter how passionate you are about it, has to provide you with a way to survive.

There are entire YouTube channels, podcasts and websites focused on "how to make money online" and I've learned a ton from them. I'm going to leave the explanation of "how" to them. I will however, give you some perspective on how I make a living online in generalities.

I've always thought it was really important to maintain multiple streams of income, and when creating content online, it's essential. This is because of how volatile and ever changing online business can be. YouTube could change it's payout method, or completely shutdown tomorrow. Someone could hijack your account and ruin your search engine standing. There are a million things that are completely out of your control. By spreading your eggs to many different baskets, you minimize the impact that any one of them can have on you if it were to disappear. Some of the ways that I bring in income are product sales (digital plans, t-shirts, stickers, etc.), Patreon support (ongoing crowdfunding), website ad sales, affiliate programs and YouTube ads. The largest of them, by FAR, is sponsorship.

Some people equate sponsorship with selling out, and generally I don't care to try to convince those people otherwise. For me personally, I handle sponsorships in this way.

One of my main goals with my business in general is to provide value to my viewers. If a brand who makes a quality product, and could provide value to my viewer wants to sponsor me, I'll consider it. If the product is not quality, or doesn't add value, I pass. Value, in this case, is pretty broad. I work with a mattress company as a sponsor, and while that may not seem like a direct value add for my viewers, in my mind it is. That's because I personally tell my friends about how much the product improved my sleep. I would do that whether they paid me or not. Plus, everyone has to sleep, right?

What a lot of viewers don't see is how many sponsorship opportunities get turned down by me and other creators on a regular basis. As a creator, you WILL be courted by companies who want to give you money. Be very careful to value that money against the cost of promoting another company that you have no stake in. It's a fine line, and I do have some sponsorships that I wish I hadn't taken. Even the ones that ended up not being a great fit, taught me more about how to vet opportunities that come in.

Initially, I reached out to a couple of companies that I wanted to try to work with. I had about a 50% success rate with that, but it was enough to get some income rolling. Very early on, I decided not to actively pursue companies for sponsorship unless I was willing to promote them for free anyway (i.e. a company I just REALLY, REALLY love). In my mind, if a potential sponsor approaches me, then it's because the recognize what I'm doing, and find it valuable to them. I guess in the business world, that gives me the upper hand. In my mind, it means that I don't have to convince them. It's also much easier to say "no, just free product isn't worth it" when they approach me. Initially, you'll likely get more offers for free product than money. Everyone has to figure out that value on their own, but my thinking is that there are very few cases where that's worthwhile for me. I can't spend a free product on food for my kids. If I'm paid by a company, I can use that money for whatever I need.

THE BIGGEST ADVICE I can give in regards to sponsorships is this: Don't feel pressured to say yes to every opportunity. Value your time, and audience more than a short term financial gain.

Once you find a sponsor, you'll be in a territory of contracts and licensing. This can be a bit overwhelming if you don't have experience reading and deciphering documents like that. My biggest suggestion here is to make sure that you and the sponsor are both extremely clear about the expectation of the other. Just like a personal relationship, if everyone's expectations are clear, it makes navigating an potential issues much easier, and removes a lot of potential misunderstanding.

Sponsorships are handled very differently by different creators. It's something that each of us have to navigate and learn by doing, just like the rest of this stuff. It's important to remember that content is king. If you focus on getting sponsorships, you'll probably have a tough time. If you focus on creating compelling, well made and valuable content, you will find an audience. Sponsors want access to your audience, so that is the first thing to build, and the thing that you need to actively maintain. Of the multiple income streams that I mentioned above, most of them are driven directly from the audience. The audience are the patrons, the website visitors, the t-shirt purchasers, the affiliate link clickers. Sponsors don't do those things. The number of eggs in the sponsorship basket can change often, so I lean on the audience driven income as a more consistent source. Value your audience first, keep them there and engaged. Sponsorships are a way for you to provide them extra value, while adding another income source.

For the first year, after I went full time, I was handling all of the sponsorship communication myself. I had to keep track of the state of all negotiations, carefully read contracts (and research the language in them) as well as actually do the work to produce the sponsored video. This was one of the biggest pain points for me at that time. In a conversation with another creator, he told me that he had a close friend who handled those conversations for him for 10% of the earnings. He said that having another person as the contact and negotiator took away a huge burden on both his time and focus. He said that when dealing with opportunities himself, his tendency was to agree to terms and pricing that weren't ideal, as a way to maintain the relationship. An agent is someone who acts on your behalf, but doesn't have to act LIKE you. They have a different investment in whether deals turn out or not. They are working FOR you and their return is based on what they bring in for you.

Based on his recommendation, I found a close friend who had some extra time to take on these communications here and there as the emails showed up. It wasn't an hourly or timed job, just a 10% commission for whatever deals closed. In an interesting turn of events, after about a week, I

got a call from a trusted talent agent who wanted the same
10%, but had an actual agency behind them with industry
contacts and history. My friend was really just trying to
help me out as a way to fill free time, so she gladly stepped
out of it (and started her own growing business!)

I certainly don't think having someone act as an agent,
friend or professional, is absolutely necessary, but for me..
it's been invaluable. Since I started working with my agent,
my time is more free to do the work that I want. My agent
has contacts and access to companies that I never would
have been able to reach on my own. I've been told that
agents only want money and don't care about the people
they represent. This may be true in general, but I genuinely
feel like mine is fighting for me and promoting me in ways
that I wouldn't have done myself. That could easily be done
by a close friend as well, as long as you trust them. Having
an agent has done a couple of things for me that have been
game changing.

Most of us, especially artists and creatives, undervalue
our work. I'm blown away when I hear my agent talk to a
company about me. He sells me like I'm the best thing in the
world, and confidently tells them what my content and my
audience is worth. Personally, I would have a really hard
time validating my worth in that way, in that setting. It
would feel like pure ego. Having someone stand in that
place has been completely worthwhile, and actually a bit
humbling. For him, it's not ego, it's sales. The separation of
me, as a person, and him as a sale representative has a bigger
effect than I realized.

For the income, our goal has been for him to always
bring in more than what I brought in on my own, even after
his 10% is taken out. Almost a year into working with him,

every single sponsorship he's managed has been far beyond what I made on my own.

On the other hand, I've talked to people who handle every bit of that themselves, love it and are very successful at it! Again, there's no ONE way to do this. If you want to run the sponsorship parts on your own, go for it (it's an extra 10% in your pocket)!

ULTIMATELY, I decided that being my own agent was one of those task I didn't want to do, like I mentioned in the "GETTING HELP" section. I'm not great at it and although it was necessary, doing the work myself was making it harder to do the work that I loved. Agents, like most other things, have contracts with end dates. It's something you can try for a period, and change or continue when the contract ends.

BEING FLUID

Expect things to change. Technology changes, the audience changes, WE change... everything changes and that's a good thing. A big thing that I try to remember as I move from project to project is that I'm constantly changing as a person, as a maker and as a content creator. If I'm not changing in those things, to at least a small degree, then I'm not growing. Those changes require you to be willing and able to adjust your processes. I've found that in the time I've been doing content creation full time, I've had to modify just about everything I do, to some degree. Sometimes that's out of necessity, sometimes it's just a way to for me integrate a new idea. If we get too set into our methods, we can miss some opportunities that require us to be flexible.

Some changes to my daily work flow are dictated by technology that I can't control, but a lot of those changes are forced, by me. I intentionally try to make small, incremental changes in my content and process to improve the over all quality of the content. I do it in small changes because the viewers are less likely to notice.

Some people like to throw a whole bunch of change into

one place and see the reaction to "EVERYTHING IS DIFFERENT NOW!!!" but for me, I'd prefer for no one to even notice that change is happening (in my content) but just find themselves enjoying it more and more, hopefully. There's no right or wrong approach here obviously. It's about preference. The important thing, I think, is to be ready to make changes to anything at any time. I've found that a good way to help that along, is to be in a constant state of learning.

Learning new skills, or information gives you more tools to use in your business. When you have more tools at your disposal, you're more likely to find ways to make things better. So, if you're constantly learning, you'll probably also be constantly improving and changing things.

Sometimes change can also mean removing things that slow you down or cause unnecessary stress. Personally, I have a tendency to want to only add rather than replace things. The number of hours in a day doesn't change for any of us but we (or at least I) want to try to accomplish more and more in those same number of hours. The reality is that eventually we all hit a physical limit and something has to give. It's a good idea, when changing and adding new things to your business, to also re-evaluate all of the things you're already doing. Are any of those things taking too much time based on their return? Are any of them causing too much stress or costing you too much?

Don't be afraid to remove things as a way of evolving your business. Sometimes pruning a plant is essential for it to grow larger and flourish.

THE BEGINNING

I did my best to write down some of the important moments of the early parts of my full time content creation journey, but I sincerely hope this is only the beginning. I HOPE to change from here.

I hope to improve and keep learning. I also hope that at least some small part of this book will give you a nudge towards doing something new, as a business, hobby or just as an experiment. I'm humbled to be able to make things that interest me for a living. I hope that I can use my experiences to motivate others to try new things and realize that they are capable of more than they think.

YOU are capable of more than you realize! You're unique, valuable and have a lot to offer the world!

I'm very grateful for your interest in my thoughts. I can't wait to see what you do next...

Now, let's get started...

GO MAKE AWESOME STUFF!

-Bob

Made in the USA
Columbia, SC
11 February 2018